WHAT WATER KNOWS

WHAT WATER KNOWS

～ POEMS ～

JACQUELINE JONES LAMON

TriQuarterly Books/Northwestern University Press
Evanston, Illinois

TriQuarterly Books
Northwestern University Press
www.nupress.northwestern.edu

Printed in the United States of America

10   9   8   7   6   5   4   3   2   1

Library of Congress Cataloging-in-Publication Data

Names: LaMon, Jacqueline Jones, author.
Title: What water knows : poems / Jacqueline Jones LaMon.
Description: Evanston, Illinois : TriQuarterly Books/Northwestern University Press, 2021.
Identifiers: LCCN 2020053495 | ISBN 9780810143845 (paperback) |
    ISBN 9780810143852 (ebook)
Subjects: LCSH: Water—Poetry.
Classification: LCC PS3612.A547 W48 2021 | DDC 811.6—dc23
LC record available at https://lccn.loc.gov/2020053495

For my fierce family—blood, marital, and chosen

CONTENTS

II. The Open, Empty Mouth

III. The Promise of Relief

I

This Fragile, Resilient Life

NO ONE EATS ICICLES ANYMORE

And it's rare to find people who drink water from a tap. People
consume with fear, put faith in labels over content, envision
the crystal springs of Detroit and the Alpine mountain tops
of Toledo from the renderings on green labels fast-glued
to plastic bottles. Someone said, *You get just what you pay for*

and someone believed that wise guy and showered him with cash.
We all know that someone. We all know the risk we take when
faucets come from nowhere seen and don't demand our daily
cash. This world once survived on our rainwater, collected
in buckets left outside our doors. Imagine. We once ran outside,

once welcomed the onslaught of weather. Imagine. We embraced
the cold, awakened to crunch and grind and snap, broke icicles away
from the rafters, and gave no thought to acid rain. Look at us—
doing better because we know so much, creating new basic needs
and flashy ways to fulfill them. We have come so far from olden days.

It only costs a dollar to quench our deepest thirsts.

She was terrified of all that it took to be free
Traversing the waters from above or below
Those bridges. These tunnels. That river. This sea.

After driving through darkness as divorcee-to-be
Although she knew this was the choice way to go
She was terrified of all that it took to be free.

She'd packed bags of nothing like an inflamed refugee
And closed her eyes to every pain she elected not to know
Those bridges. These tunnels. That river. This sea.

Tollbooths were roadblocks as far as she could see
Penniless and bleeding in this highway horror show
She was terrified of all that it took to be free.

The city, the moonlight, the blooming family tree
Were coming into focus like the water's steady flow
Those bridges. These tunnels. That river. This sea.

And once she decided, all life could agree
She could shrink into night, plunge, or choose now to grow
She was terrified of all that it took to be free
Those bridges. These tunnels. That river. This sea.

TRAVELOGUE

One morning, on my way to work, a burgundy Jeep tailed me, swerved around my sedan, then tiptoed through the stop sign. I don't think he understood the truth—I am a woman with so much at stake. That driver found my ways ridiculous, but I always brake hard, then take a full breath, look both ways before I inch into an intersection.

When I see flashing reds, my breath leaves my body and I don't know where it goes.
                                        This is how one Black woman breathes.

When I hear sirens in approach, my blood holds a pose and prays to escape detection.
                                        This is how one Black woman hears.

The morning after Rodney King, an officer believed that yellow to have been red; he walked up to my window while I screamed for him not to kill me. Please, don't kill me. I don't want to die on the way to school. I just want to be present for my Criminal Procedure exam.

When he showed me his open hands, my cheek streaked crimson, right where he could have slapped me.
                                        This is how a Black woman's skin fights back.

When he told me that he held no arms, my chest felt punctured, ribs splintered, lungs deflated.
                                        This is how a Black woman manifests the world in which she lives.

This morning, on my walk to town, I carried a folded cloth bag to hold my purchased bread, olive tapenade, squash, and cheese. I searched for something almost sweet to add, for later, for dessert. The air was still, too heavy for my memory of new language; my identification sewn into the

French seam of my past. There is only room left for tiny chocolates in a tote of this size. A wise woman eats to thrive.

This is how a Black woman travels with herself. Always with herself, and the trail of all her selves.

The possibility, the threat.

WHAT HAPPENS WHEN A BROTHER FLEES
for Ballie Crutchfield

I don't want to see their faces. Don't want hatred
be my final vision of this simple, kindred life.

Not their hands in need around my neck, their spittle
slimed and weighty on my sweating skin,

their torches held high above their heads, creating
smoke signs on this full moon night. A crow caws.

Those who would want to come knew not to come,
knew to hide their kin, say a prayer, secure

what they could bolt and hope that it would hold.
When I asked what I had done, some voice hollers—

*You were born
into a clan of animals.*

This been my simple life. And simple is not easy.
Simple is the Round Lick Creek below this bridge,

the bend of trees, the symphony of water
finding its way through leaves, twigs, rocks,

and the messy remains of life. This one tells me
to look into his eyes, shotgun barrel

hard pressed into the bridge of my nose, tell him
what I see. Can't speak. I want to see my fireflies.

I want to see my mother. I want to see the water
rush between my fingers, so cool and full of song.

Who knows the crime. Who knows
the truth. Hold him down. Convict him.
Shackle his ankles. Lock him up for life.

Send him up. Rehab him. Check his pen.
Let him write to that teacher. Watch her save
those scrambled letters. He will tell her of Allah,

what he thinks he did to get there,
what will never change. She will write
him back. They'll slice her letters into cryptic

adjectives and occasional conjunctions.
He will inject meaning: She cut him out.
She ain't down to visit. Shit, he knew it all

along. He sings in Sing Sing. He dances
in Dannemora. He curses the reasoning
of his jagged life. He takes on a guard.

He dies for the death. Send a suit for his home-
going. Don't hold your breath. The Hudson
slows in the winter months, thicker in the cold.

"GOVERNOR SNYDER DRINKS FLINT WATER"

They say someone has to drink this stuff.
Someone has to take a sip. They remind me
it's been purified, the lead removed, and all

is well, but still. As the camera rolls, I fixate
on the crimson dot, on *action*. I think of karma,
the revenge of gods and gangsters, my body's betrayal—this thirst.

When I look at this family seated on the couch
I see endless layers of offspring who'll crave chips
of peeling paint. There's Baby-Sister Deficit,

near Mother Shift-the-Blame. *Action. Say something.
There once was a problem, but it's all been fixed.* I pick
up the glass, seal my lies around the rim, pray

away osmosis. They say to look as if I am drinking,
exhale as though refreshed. Maybe ask for seconds. Exit
with my sheepish grin, two jugs filled up from the tap.

PIPELINE

The most direct path between two points
is not always the straightest line. A path
that travels through the earth can disrupt
spirit, can displace our core. How can you
not know this? How can you not place
the soles of your feet on the soil of this ground
and not become more of your best self?

There are other ways. There is the air
of wisdom, of elders who studied cause
and the source of least resistance, who
thrived and built a people without also
destroying a world. But this is what you
know—to claim as yours all that you see

and destroy what came before you. Look
at my damaged eyes, swollen from your non-
lethal pepper spray attacks, over and over
again. Look at the wounds on my legs, the dog
bites that I will never allow to heal. I am
so reminded of you, of your thirst so insistent,
your greed and your greed and your greed.

May we not die for white convenience. May
we not succumb to the infiltration of poisons
into and onto our land. May we stand and
not suffer the disruption of all that is sacred,
the burials, the graves, the artifacts of survival.
May we no longer be slaughtered because
we are standing, so vocal and very alive.

LEMONADE
for Jennie Steers

Someone shouts, *Make Her Say It*, and it rises up
like anthem, all those voices clashing in the light.
Makes me think about humanity, how we try
to make sense of the senseless—the twisted cord
of living—dividing what's perfect in two.

In the center of this swarm of men
is a tightly fisted heart, beating faster
than a hummingbird's, wildfire
taking flight. Someone here
is enraged enough to know the truth
—there was no poisoned lemonade—
just a long, slow sip of too much summer, a girl
seeking solace on my porch, her confession
of transgression, my promise not to tell.

I am eyeing this bulbous crowd and these sheets
on my line, billowing shade and shadow, the teakettle
screeching for all manner of swelling to halt.

The one man who should thank me most is he
who'll take me down, drag me over, hoist me up.

Someone's husband.

Someone's father.

Someone's living, breathing son.

MOB

It wants what it wants before its people know the wanting.

I hide in a cavern carved out beneath floorboards, ask my skin
to do my breathing. I've always thought my greatest threat
to be pests I could not see—the termites and the carpenter ants,
the mammals who burrow and wait. In this makeshift shelter, I hear terror—
the phlegmy breath of a child who shares my darkness.

He is the boy of another, a skittish new voice in my safe space.
He coughs, curses, calls those charging toward us *animals*—
but the animals I've come to know embrace tender
within reason, even in the face of senseless slaughter.

No, this is the underside of evil's impetus, the reason
we all need to pray to something beyond a notion—
the creator of eclipse,
the holder of the hurricane,
the supplier of our sustenance—
the instiller of wretched fever that keeps the furious and misguided
temporarily close to home.

I pray for our miracle—*Dear God, please* . . .

Someone kicks open the door
to my shed. Someone stands above
me. Someone waits and listens.

A hound trots, sniffs, barks—
scratches the hover above my head.

Someone calls out to the others.

SIX

The Children's March, 1963

The water pressure from a fire hose
can stop a moving bullet, can ransack
a door wedged shut, and extinguish
any embers, including those we cannot
see. Bull saw us all as threat—the lot
of us, the endless stream that poured
out of our church and onto the street.
We sang and we held hands. We held
onto our purpose—to be true to our God,
true to our native land, to Birmingham,
like the thirsty sponges we were. We
sang a song we'd practiced and knew
by heart. We were not letting anyone turn
us around, turn us around, turn us around.
I was six and needed something more
than what I thought I knew, a freedom
song, a choice of where to play,
of who could teach me lessons, the very
content of my dreams of what I wanted
to be when I grew up, if I grew up,
when I grew up and took my very next
breath. But let's get back to that bullet,
stopped by an unequal force, confronted
by mere droplets corralled into sinister
duty. I heard those dogs before I saw them
—growls, snarls—trained to see nothing
of my size, my gentleness. I knew the water
in the air just before it launched me airborne,
ramming me into disbelief, then tree trunk,
then a crowded mass of children's hips and legs.
I was six and my song ordained that I be seen
as change, or silenced, arrested and contained.
I had lost my shoes and my blue hair ribbons.

I was wearing a muddy crinoline and learned
the coolness of both iron bars and the beady
eyes of hatred, a jailer's sputum gelling
on the side of my face that I refused to touch.

NIAGARA

Annie Edson Taylor was the first person to survive
the trip over Niagara Falls in a barrel.

She was a widowed schoolteacher and made the trip
on October 24, 1901—her sixty-third birthday.

I. The Queen of the Mist: Annie Edson Taylor

This is how you do it—you think of yourself
as a part of the current. You, as creator of turbulent

diversion. You, the spark of white water
crest in pursuit of all things blue and green.

I'd gone there before, heard myself within
that constant roar in a way I'd never known.

All of that crashing. All of that motion. And me.
I stood on the shore, questioned my part in the trine.

And the answers came—how I could take my life
into my own hands and live with fierce abandon.

I could fling myself to save myself, take the nuttiest
notion on the path to steadying my later years. Yes.

I could see myself floating. I could feel myself fall.
I could smell all that moisture. I had nothing to lose.

◆ ◆ ◆

When people think of my journey, they think of my fall,
But what I remember most is my emergence, the sawing

through the barrel, straight through to the back of my head.
When asked would I repeat my past, I think back forty years

to my mother and father, my siblings, my life, elite education,
what remained ever mine in the bank. All of my choices packed

in this wooden sphere—my dead husband and my dead son, my tarnished
silver spoon. It seems as if I have always been gasping for air, seeking

to place my memories right side up, preparing my table
for influential guests that always left too soon. You should know

that every piece of my silver is sterling, and when I see my reflection,
I smile at the woman I see. I am *Mrs.* Taylor. I am a teacher of charm.

I can convince a snake-oil salesman that carney has nothing on me.
I am the next wild attraction all the people will pay to see.

◆ ◆ ◆

◆ ◆ ◆

I will not take that plunge again, and neither, my friend,
should you. Given the choice, I would rather face the cannon's

force than to try the falls once more. And what would be
the purpose? What would there be to gain? I look around

and wonder—what man would push me over the edge
of the rowboat, seal my lid, and provide me with enough air

to breathe until I surface? Who is there to take the risk,
to give me what I need? The authorities said if I didn't survive

all who helped would stand trial for my death. But what if
I survive, a second time? Who will stand trial for my life?

I can see it now, the headline—*Mild-Mannered, Spinster
Schoolteacher Delights a Most Terrified Crowd*. The spectator

ladies will turn their heads away; the children will cover their eyes.
But the men will bet good money and some of those present will win.

In 1995, Steve Trotter and Lori Martin were the first
male-female duo to survive the falls.

Martin was a "last minute replacement"
for another unnamed woman.

This section is written in the anonymous woman's voice.

II. *The Maid of the Mist: The Bad Boy's First Selection*

I thought there was nothing I wouldn't do for him,
this tall mass of muscles and wavy, sun-bleached hair.

I wanted all his danger, his push-me-pull-me dance,
to sneak into the movies, hot-wire his neighbor's car.

My mother laughed when she met him, pinched his butt
when we rang in the new. And this is what he told me—

That she was exceptionally cool, then patted the top
of my head while she chain-smoked his unfiltered cigs.

But then he brought me my Frye's—blood red, with bold
stitching in beige, in a size just a tad bit too tight. *You want*

'em to stay on your feet when you fly . . . And the image remained
in the back of my brain—the two of us running away, taking

flight; the two of us climbing the high peaks of the world;
drawing attention in red cowboy boots, living our maverick lives.

✦ ✦ ✦

◆ ◆ ◆

I don't know when it happened—everything I did became the exact
wrong thing to do, every word an incendiary twig. He seemed to be

distracted, as though my words were a dialect too distant
to understand, my emotions too foreign a language to read. It was

our winter of blazing hot ice, with his laser focus on top-secret
things, and my gaze fixed on nothing at all. He was my living

fun house, my gargoyle come to life. And yet, I loved the stone
of him, the way he gleamed from spit-shine sex, calcifying

my dreams every night. My brothers asked to kick his ass, said I could
do better than that. No one could access his marrow like me.

On Valentine's Day, I drove to his house. I'd baked him a pineapple
ham. When he opened the door, he was holding a beer. He said,

What the hell? slammed it shut. My mother said sweetness
yields better results, said I should have baked him a cake.

◆ ◆ ◆

◆ ◆ ◆

Two weeks after Easter, I pick up the phone. Yeah, it's him,
and he says he's got news. He hurt me real bad but his voice

got me good and I wanted to hear what he'd say. He told me
he missed me. He said he was wrong. He asked if I loved him.

I told him I did. That's how it begins—how the ending unfurls.
My world spun off-center and centered on him, what he needed

and wanted and wished. Would I do anything, to get my man
back? He asked me and I said I would. I thought he meant,

you know, something between us, or us and a good friend
of ours. That night he arrived and we drove to this barn

a few counties over from mine. He said, *Now's your chance
to be famous with me*, and I saw this contraption, this time-travel

shit, and I knew he meant dying for him. I smiled, feigned
excitement, and just backed away, not knowing what else I could do.

III. *The Hornblower: The Woman on the Edge*

He tells me, *This is not a romantic trip, just a sight-*
seeing tour, and I get in the rental and drive us to the falls.

He employs me. He implores me. He leaves me
wanting more. And I look back over my shoulder of years,

the weight of possibility causing everything in me to slump
and hope and wait for him to offer up his overtime, anything

to blur the line between our working days and next. I take
what I can get—his midnight rants about what his wife won't

do, his early morning wake-up calls, those heady lists of errands
that keep me by his side. He names today, *Diversion*—our break

in a week full of his meetings, with our single, shared room
and our lone, king-sized bed. I name this week, *Our Ontario*.

I drive well below the limit. I mimic the river's path. I roll
down all the windows. I am current, almost raging, always mist.

◆ ◆ ◆

When we stand there, he asks questions—*How many gallons
of water per sec?* Then, *See anyone we might know?* And I

think what it might mean if I were to leave him, right now,
in this space, then straddle the fences and jump. I wonder how

long it would take for the plunge, how long it would take
to be missed. Those are the questions that don't leave my lips,

but whirlpool inside until there's no air to breathe and I can't
find a way to survive. How did this happen to someone like me?

A professional woman with smarts? I own my own home. I pay
my own way. I set goals and I follow through. And yet, here

I am, on this edge looking down, and measuring life without
him. I reach for his hand and he pulls it away—then again,

and again. And I'm through. I say, *What does it matter, who's
here and who's not?* But he cannot hear me over the crash.

◆ ◆ ◆

I become someone much less than myself, in the presence
of one who needs more. After a while, I can look down without

swooning, feeling dizzy, or yielding to pain. I focus on those jagged
rocks, wonder how they endured all these years with the steadiest

onslaught of force. I need something nutritious to eat. All
of this water and still I feel thirst—I know I need something

to drink. This is the role that I have accepted to play. I am
the woman who stands on the edge between giving and needing

to want. He says, *That's who we are—you and me—a good
time*. And I think of the eyes of his wife. I think of his phone

calls to her in the night, his need for my silence, my peace.
They say almost half of the people who jump here are women,

twice as high as you'll find somewhere else. It's not romantic,
it's just what it is—just diversion, just a stop on the way.

OWNERSHIP

And this is what you need from me—the mark
of my hand on this tall stack of papers, initials
at the *X*, full signatures where the arrows point,
my name printed all in full caps. There is a plane
to catch, a tapping foot, a tuition check to write.
Reminder to self: Remember the faces
of your sons and your daughter. There is no water
in this desert, no water in this glass, no time for me
to swallow. I don't remember how that pen appears,
but here it is—just like the notary now seated
at our dining room table, opposite me
and smiling. She says she does this all the time,
quit claims to get the cash, deeds it back once
the refinance goes through, how everyone stands
to gain. It is just a quick matter of paperwork, boxes
to check, a single queue to navigate, a tiny fee to pay.

WHAT IS HUMAN, OR CULTURE,
OR LEFT HANGING IN THE AIR

Oh, I'm sure he was only kidding . . . And I take that in,
my reaction to his statement held up as my noir faux
pas, my inability to take a joke, to see more into this
than you are sure was intended, my prickly skin far
too thin to be of good use in this new locale. I think

now of what it means to *marry up*, to do well by social
climb, to become what one should strive to be,
if ever given the choice. Tonight, you sit at this table
and eat of my food. Tonight, you compliment me
on what I've prepared, say how much you can taste the love

in this dish, pause for me to please offer you more. And each
day at this table, I await invitation—thin slice of your cheese,
those crackers with mustard you say *I simply must try*,
but never prepare for my plate. How demurely we smile
when we're ever so full, then demand that the other should ask.

New Jersey. Mississippi. The southern segment of France.

ALL THAT WE NEED TO BE HAPPY

It is that time at the end of the day, that time after lunch

and before the night rush when the hostess will seat us

without checking our names and give us a moment to take

off our coats. Today, all we want is a table for two, a place

in the corner away from the noise, an outlet to recharge,

to plug in our lives. A moment. Our moment. Some fries

or some chips. But first, she sets down a brown bottle and glass,

a setup, a menu and asks what we will have. And then

we look up at our server and smile, *I'll stick with the water,*

and watch her smile fade. *Well, you know drinks are half price,*

at least until six? And we nod and acknowledge the unspoken

truth—the sheer mathematics of our liquid restraint,

how our choice of beverage seems less than ideal—the bare

bones, the cheap choice, the group think gone bad.

ON WATCH FOR THE SPONTANEOUS

After contractions and after the blood, after the comings
and goings of staff, after the changing of volunteer shifts,
the wiping of brow and the squeezing of hands, a specialist says
what we should expect: the thinnest blue skin and still growing hair.

And so, the monitor is removed so you may die without
witness. There's no amniotic pillow to cushion your free fall.
The doctors know—this one grips my shoulder, tells me
to be strong—none of this undoing will truly take that long.

And they administer Pitocin into the IV.
And they say it will progress and this pain and this rush
and the landslides cull life as you cling to my roots
and my branches, refusing to let go. And they

increase the dosage while you and I both cleave to slabs
and cracks that none of them can see. *There are benefits
to funeral rites*, the social worker says, to naming
you and carving your name in stone. And, no—I cannot

imagine that day in conjunction with this night—
this absence of water, that absence of light. Their will be
done, they say. They send us home to salvage something
of what we could have been. They send us home to wait.

THE GARONNE RIVER SHIFTS HER DIRECTION

So perhaps I made it all up—that these cannons sound
to break the heaviest of clouds, eliminate the yin
and yang that birth the lightning, and the thunder
that's sure to follow. When I share this story, it makes
no sense, I know. I, too, envision one single man

in a worn, floppy hat, running to restock artillery
in fourteen-second increments, to keep us all
storm-free. As though this is all it takes to rule
the weather. As though any one of us could be
the reason that lightning strikes another of us

down. And yet, here I am and here we are, listening
to roosters now crow, to the birds in flight resume
their chirp of the day. You and I are alive and well,
safe within our structures. This, so absurd—one man
in a hat, a figment at best, remnant of every lost dream.

Nuclear power. A howl in the distance. The absence of afternoon bees.

CLASSIFICATION IS THE BEGINNING
OF OUR GREATEST UNDERSTANDING

What must you do when your needs fill you with the greatest
level of distaste? Let's say that your tap tastes like mercury,
and so, you refuse to drink. Let's name this *The Metallic Effect,*
so you will know exactly what we mean—chilling, sharp, and jagged.
It is a phenomenon, and so we could call it that—*The Deadly Thirst*

Phenomenon, because it follows us around, like a mosquito
intent on sharing yellow fever or whatever she may have
in store. Except the mosquito never thinks this way. This train
of thought is man-made, at best—the insect only wanting
what she knows she needs to survive. After the bite, we render

a punishment that is nothing short of death. Before it, we stand
around their habitats, then complain about our discomfort.
But I digress—and this digression, too, is a part of the whole,
the way we loop around and loop around the thing until
we find all our options far too brittle and tangled to unfurl.

The schoolgirls. The pedophile. The coyote's moonlit wails.

NINE TO THE LIMIT

No one understands why the limit is so low,

thirty with no lights in sight, just Call-a-Head,

the portables place on the right. And no one

wants to go there, unless that is where they have

to go. In a quarter mile, it will shift to forty.

It seems so far away. But everyone knows

you add nine to the limit—ten might yield

a ticket, if you're no native to this no-man's-

land. Even with the added nine, they zoom

zippy at the stretch—Jamaica Bay before you,

wildlife preserve flanking your sides—fast

lane taken away to have a designated place

to sweep all this carnage—seagulls fallen

from the sky, a random raccoon flattened,

a cyclist who couldn't survive an eighteen-

wheeler's passing, nipped in the bike lane

and propelled into spin. On summer nights,

they flash cheesy neon skeletons, say there's reason

for the numbers, for why they're so dang low.

Some driver hit a utility pole, downed a sturdy

shade tree at least two stories tall. They say

that guy was twenty-three, in a hurry to get

from here to there, in a hurry to cross

the bridge and get to the other side. Kid made

a choice we'd never make. Probably sang to stolen

music, took yellows urine stale. Or dude

was noticing an unmarked while scoping out

his rearview—driving drunk while texting,

but hell, no one knows for sure.

PRODIGAL

I don't know where you've been. It's been days since I've seen you last, one hour running into the next until I can't tell where one night ends and another season begins. That is my story, the place where my words take shape. Your story is your body and your body has brought you back here.

Your skin is cool and moist. I search for the right thing to say.

Sallow, streaked with the grime of what tries to remain hidden but never can for long—subways, doorways, vestibules. You smell like any man without water or air. Toxicity is still sniffing your trail, chasing you, and hunting you down.

You are. You are here and you are now.

We take what we can get sometimes. This night, there is the sound of the ocean's surf—the crash that is soothing the shore. I point out the blues of the boardwalk—and then the stars, the satellites, the planes attempting to land. The beauty we are offered. The beauty we choose to accept.

You tell me I don't get it. Your eyes are darker than my memory paints them, your expression vacant and impossible to read.

I wonder if this is how it feels to perform a soliloquy in a language no one remembers.

I focus on tomorrow, the tasks that need to be performed by us, by you. All of your jeans are ripped at the crotch, once again. I need to take you shopping. I need to learn your measurements. I need to do what I know to do to fix this fraying fabric.

I want to die, you monotone. You take a deep drag on your cigarette, hold it in forever. *To feel something. Anything at all.*

I touch your arm. We walk. You look like a standing ovation to me.

THE BROWNING

Bricks scream. It is the hottest day of the year, and this is saying something. It is saying that the air is a suicidal Mobius strip around itself and the inhabitants of the city are caught up in the tightening. No one gives a damn about decorum anymore; one quick glance at apartment building windows at dusk tells nothing but the truth, if the truth is there to be told. The women and the men walk around without covering, their heads tilted back in reverence to the ceiling fans that only suggest relief. Everyone sweats and smells of themselves. The body becomes a bundle of rising. The body becomes a rippling pool of bettering. The body melts and overtakes the last drop of water in the world. This is a fact, predicted on the internet. Tonight, the city will try to save what little is left of the grid and the grit. The news anchors will still go to work. Those kids will still dance on the motionless trains. But other than that, the difference looms large. The planners and plotters will turn down the dial, encourage our stillness, squirrel away all the power they can.

II

THE OPEN, EMPTY MOUTH

WE COULD WALK INTO THE WATERS,
OR LEAVE LIFE AS IT SEEMS

This one good eye of mine creates definitives,
lines of demarcation between the sky and the sea,
the ocean and the beyond. I have no depth perception.
My ever-after begins right here, right now, every day.
It's all such illusion ::You:: over there, doing this work
you have been given to do
and me:: in this space, doing mine.

I can smell saltwater.

Some would say there are no oceans between us, only
land. I would say it all depends on the direction we choose
to face. If you look above your head, you may see containers
and rafters, unbalanced, poised to fall. And, if I choose that pose,
I might see darkness hiding clouds in drift, and stars.
Tonight, I am hoping for fireflies. Tonight, you
are waiting for thunder, an early departure, then rain.

THERMOSTAT

He says I shouldn't need it, the arctic

manufactured chill I turn on in the heat.

It is over a hundred degrees now

and this is the blizzard inside our lives.

His friends nod along, watch him storm away

from the thermostat set to his liking,

our children lethargic, dreaming of snow.

My mind drifts, skates over memories where

my voice falls through thin patches, my body

numb and freezing. There are things I don't say,

my body and brain a mush of hot ice

that burns before it takes the hint and melts.

It comes down to a snowball's chance in hell—

that wall of aprons puddled, just beyond the gates.

They say it's an issue of taxes. They say be glad
things turned out as they did, that you would owe
more than you own, that you would be all
upside down and floundering to find air with water
all around you. They, who have never seen you

swim. They, who measure the world by an arm's
length around them, needing hardware to verify
being. Your mothers live well beneath waterfalls,
your aunts make do in coral reefs. You are at home
and in search of the house that no man's signature

will ever take away. Your dreams take shape just beyond
French doors. Your actions—seen through leaded panes
of beveled, stained-glass windows. And there you stand,
in one of the many rooms of your choosing, writing
the check for the balance, being and being and being.

The offer. The acceptance. The new consideration.

WITH A VIEW OF THE WATER FROM STABLE, CLEARED GROUND

There are houses to be owned in Kingston, an incredible number
of houses that work, once you know what it is that you need.
Picture this . . . There you are—turning your key and stepping inside,
sleeping upstairs, and paying the mortgage on time. You write
on your sunporch, sip chamomile tea, listen to the swish of leaves

in your spacious yet humble backyard. In Kingston,
your life is affordable. In Kingston, almost all pieces fit.
The CVS carries the lipstick you wear and the pizza is cheesy
and hot. The Hudson River dances all along the eastern edge,
while people dance inside the pubs. If only your students

would all move up there, take over a classroom near
that quaint little diner, turn in their assignments online.
If only the world would render one good cosmic shake—OK,
two or three to be sure, and allow you to stand there,
your deed in your hands, your happy, smart car in the drive.

Hurricane Sandy. The '94 Quake. The I-14, all covered with ash.

You are doing the best that you can, and for this, we can all be grateful. When you rise, you rise above imbalance; when you sleep, you sleep despite the lure of the ever-racing heart. You partner with our world each day, sweeping in and dipping, creating allusions to a harrowing life, and a health we hold up as hope. We have learned to embrace these contradictions, to take the day on its own spiraled terms. You have taught me this. I am awake and dreaming this is restful sleep. I am crossing the street while waiting for you on the other side. In the heat wave, you set the air at sixty degrees, wrap your sleeping self in layers of linens, then sweat until heat turns into cool, and cool transforms the swelter. We get up when we can. And when we do, we call it our good morning.

THE NIGHT BEFORE EUTHANASIA

There will be a time when the body
cannot do what the body needs to do.

When it holds the scent of mercury
in nail beds and scalp
and the back of knee, despite us all.

I remember the scent of death, on and around
my mother—less metallic and more
like heavy sweet cream, so altered,

a species apart—and still—the smell
was death and dead and dying—yes,

I know it now. We know it when
we take it in, the saccharin slap
of next and next, the memory we are

born with, forever intact. Tonight,
my dog walks in endless circles,

dripping labyrinths of blood and urine,
his hope to find an appropriate end.
Did I give him all he needs for this?

He lets me hold him, nods as though I am
saying something he understands.
I am silent. All I can do is breathe

against the heave of his breath.
So shallow. So little. So cut. He staggers
with the center of his back peaked

like the camel he wished himself to be—a traveler
across the barren land of a living room,
en route. Around in a circle, again and again,

the circumference growing smaller
and smaller and smaller still, until
there is nowhere else to turn

and everything stands
so very, very still.

WHAT WE WEAR TO MEET THE WATER
Aboard the Hudibras, 1786

I heard they threw them naked, overboard, handing down sackcloth
from the dead to the dying. I named the dead's clothing for the spirits
they once contained and I knew it was true—how the body wasn't bound
by the outer surfaces of the skin, but took up residence in fibers, too.
A life next to a life clings to a life, if only to tattle on the intricacies.

We saw she'd taken ill, wouldn't eat or drink for days, just pray.
And when we came up to the deck, she was there on all fours,
her head facedown on her hands, moaning a prayerful song.
And I wailed a prayer, too, a high-pitched holler that called
out to our sisters to circle our dying one and usher her home.

We wrapped around and around—the youngest circled next to her,
the elders nearest the sea. We stood in silence until her moans
subsided, then picked up the chant when her body grew still.
We sang the songs we knew to sing. We sang the songs she taught us.
And those jailers let two of us stay, just that time, to witness the ripple

her slight body made, so we could tell others she was never exposed.

CLEANSING MY MOTHER'S COLD BODY

Someone would have to do it, but I knew that it couldn't be me.
I was her only daughter, her only child, her closest kin. For nights,
I dreamed the expression she would have made when men unzipped
her body bag, lifted her onto that metal without warming
it first. They might eat a sandwich then. They might call it a night.

They were professionals. They did this all the time. They would say
she cannot feel temperature anymore. And I would wonder where she was
and what she knew of light and humidity and circulating air, if all that
knowledge leaves us and we have to begin again. She would have nothing
on—this woman with three closets full of good things she can't wear anymore

and she would be alone in this chill without anyone with her and I
didn't know the new rules in this convoluted world of death. And no one
would tell me what I needed to know. I had taken off her earrings and put them
on my ears. I had kissed her on her cheeks, moisturized her lips. I had told her
that I loved her, that I would, one day, be OK. But I couldn't decide

what she'd want for all eternity—the muumuu, the sackcloth, the shroud . . .

THE MERCHANT SEAMAN'S WIFE

These days, I'm spending time and pocketing
the change. In the afternoons, the sun hits strong,
reminds me of my need for warmth, my life
absent of caress. These long, silent, luscious days.
On schedule, I walk to the docks, sit with my back

unsupported, imagine the hour of his return. I wonder
if I will want him—his hands sure to be stiffened,
and calloused, snagging against what I've strived
to keep taut, his vision of me a conjured oasis,

his legs unaccustomed to the dance we once learned
to do on land. This time, it's been eight months
of single plates and coffee cups, smoothing my side
of our bed—not the first time, not the last. The hard
part is reentry—this coming and going, like tide.

Imported spices. Foreign cars. Our Indonesian clothes.

ROCKAWAY

This is not a poem about the sea,
about the shore and how it changes.
Not the shifts that take place over ages,

the erosion of rock, or the nuance
of what washes up the next beach over,
belly up and flailing in its panic.

Not the seasonal tug-of-war between
summer and next, how temperature
destroys as it seeks to sustain. We know

all of that—what comes and goes
and what remains—the broad strokes
of aqua days, the tumbling of hours

into something as indigo as darkness.
How deep can we plunge and still discern
the finest shades of difference? Today,

the sea presents us with waves worthy
of riding, shoving us away on the surface,
while reeling us home with its fierce

undertow. The surfers will need this,

but maybe not us. Tomorrow, only

gulls will interrupt the smooth

of morning, the ocean parading

as lake, the argument between shore

and sea settled, if only for the moment.

If only for as long as the clouds stay

wispy overhead. The surfers will gather

to curse the calm, hands on hips in wet

suits, waiting for what others prayed

would stay away. Someone shoots

the breeze, but maybe not us. Next time,

we'll walk the shore, give names to birds,

breathe and feel each other's breath,

this salty mist on every solid thing.

AND ALL THE REST WILL HAVE WASHED AWAY

Forget that off-the-cuff advice. What makes the union
viable is a memory of slights that functions like a sieve,
a colander only fit for rinsing uncut melons, huge holes

to lose the tiny bits of bitter. You rinse until the rinds
of ripened fruit shine, leaving nothing but sweetness behind.
The unified couples know this and dance in the rain, dousing

themselves to make their skins super slick, their prickly points
softened to a malleable pulp. And here we thought it was all about
resilience, as though conviction were the stuff to yield longevity,

as though umbrellas were actually our friends. We knew so little
about what we needed to survive—a morning cup of coffee,
a nightly cup of tea, and a circle of people who respected

our joy. That, and our two-person dance over time. Maybe not
a pas de deux, maybe not a hustle. You could have been Gene
Kelly. I might have played your muse. We could have loved

the rain, the chill, and laughed while soaking wet.

QUIET ON THE SET

In real life, someone is always shouting
over someone else in order to be heard.

On the set, we are a mass of silent acquiescence.
We are a single, pliable lump of clay. We are told
that there is never a reason to approach a principal,
those actors endowed with crafted lines and recorded
mouths through which to speak. In viewers' minds,
we speak words, too—just beyond a discernable
volume, just beyond their power to hear.

In real life, the one who shouts the loudest, interrupts
with the greatest gusto, is king of the middle of the street.

On the set, we are style and the embodiment
of content. We are a couple out for cocktails, at last,
tired at week's end and grateful for this respite.
We are parents of two toddlers. We eat the steak
and the salmon, over and over again. We pass
on the dessert. Our fingers brush and linger, every take.
The director loves our energy. We haven't said a thing.

In real life, we give ourselves the most important business.
Someone will react to this, provide us with our next line.

STILL LIFE

At first, it was a family of pigeons that visited each morning,
then took up residence on the balcony, beneath the folded
table and chairs, stacked loosely in a corner. Our neighbor,

June, had died of the virus, and none of those birds perched
on her railing. My dog clawed at our storm door, growled
at the interlopers who paid him no mind, even when I stood

and watched. They eyeballed me back, daring me to challenge
their right to squawk. The streets were still. There were no
cars, no sirens, no people to be seen. Just those flocks of birds—

parcels of crows and pheasants and sparrows. Our porter,
Carlos, had died of the virus, and the birds only multiplied,
bringing more of their kind. My dog jumped at the door

handle, and I helped him to get outside. There, in the corner,
beneath a plastic folded chair, was the carcass of a large
decayed fish, a high-rise buffet for the evening crowd to come.

That day was every day—a sunrise, a sunset, an endless span
of silence. Victor, our super, wore an N95 and removed the fish
without charge. Then, Geri, our neighbor, she died, too.

POLAR VORTEX

From this sixth-floor apartment, the windows
frame our lives. Not just negative windchill
they're screaming about—how the world should take
cover, come in from outside, stay alive.
I am grateful for perspective, grateful
for canines who don't crave the cold, who do
what they can to go where they must. No one
is looking both ways. Chimneys are smoking
a pack and a half. Every blue day
we wait for the boy who's blowing his horn,
playing what we thought we knew. This is fugue.
This is what we want to hear—harmonics
to remind us we're mortal, a single
pane away from exposure in the night.

MY BODY SPEAKS OF HATRED

I've heard a spigot is here for me, somewhere near the abandoned
barn, close to the hillside field of waist-high, yellow wildflowers
I've always been afraid to cross. Here, the bees
are so heavy with themselves that they hover by my ankles,
never knowing the tops of trees, of anything an exponent
of their vision or their weight. I've spent so many days waiting
for their sting, my muscles tensed to the brink of reaction, only
asking when it will arrive and how long I'll feel the painful swell.

I will walk around the world to find another way to water.

WATER, WATER EVERYWHERE, BUT HOW AM I TO DRINK?

None of it makes any sense, how I can stand there
on the stage, look out among the crowd with ease,
make eye contact with every face, never break my gaze.
I can read a speech or give a talk, answer questions
and engage, but when it comes time to clear my throat

then take a sip of water, these hands shake so,
the water spills with all the world there watching.
I know, I know—it makes no sense—this need
for unseen quenching, to sip in secret, not be judged
by the ways I swallow water. Plastic bottles, goblets,

cups—the vessel doesn't matter. The whole world
pauses, takes a break, while I slurp and gulp and guzzle.
Convince me I can scrap the spill, that I won't create a mess.
It makes no sense to point to needs simpatico with mine,
rationalize that we all thirst and gratify my longing . . .

MARTINI

For years, we craved the highest proof—that we were
able to hold onto life. Our liquor. Our kohl. A red stain
on our lips. We could totter, pivot on the balls of our feet
and never lose our balance. We were our own fine line,

never crossed. Not that we recall/admit. During college,
the package store would deliver through the wildest
of snowstorms, taking our cash or a rubbery check
for a blind eye and the wave of a college ID. I was still

sixteen. There is so much I am sure I have forgotten—
the conjugation of irregular Portuguese verbs, that man
who wanted more for me than I wanted for myself.
Our love was on the rocks, watered down by my callousness.

He could have been the one, that almost dentist with soft
man eyes, goose laugh. Or the tall, slim-jim guy who danced
like an arm flailing tube man, knew it, and adored my slight
indifference. When we drank, there was no water anywhere,

nothing to dilute the buzz, room-temp Bacardi and Coke,
two decks of cards, last year's bus schedule, our radios
on high. Ladies, be damned—we were grown women doing
shots, holding firm to car door handles and airtight alibis.

I didn't understand my mother then. Her need of drink,
her want of need, her thirst for thirsty men. One night,
I met her at the opening of a swank Manhattan bar,
requested my first of several dirty martinis, straight

up, extra olives. She laughed herself off of the stool,
she and that bartender and that random guy who just
would not mind his business. She laughed herself silly,
laughed until the cows came home, the moon set

over Miami, and the porcelain throne became my new best
friend. She died so long ago. What we know now is how
to hold our breath, lean back, and trust that we will float.
Someone called a car for us. Someone came and took us home.

III

The Promise of Relief

THE LATITUDE, THE LONGITUDE, AND A THIRD AXIS CALLED TIME

When you change your environment, you change
your opportunities—or so said my son, endorsing
our move across the nation to a place he didn't know.
And we went, and worlds shifted, and we thought
him so wise, to have sensed that only parts of our thinking

were true, the rest only habit, relentless and dogged.
We were silent through Texas, the sky shouting
with thunder, pounding our van with hard rain.
There is a point to all weather, exclamation to recall.
Generations before, folks were warned to stay

away from windows, lest lightning strike and capture
the image of fear embedded in that pane for all eternity.
They would sit as stoics in the parlor, turn off all the lights.
They would be—together—silent, still, and calm. Prepared
for those encroaching storms, holding hands and breathing.

The desert scorch. The flooded streets. The minefields of the night.

SOCRATIC

The students know the agenda. When I step
inside our classroom, the PowerPoint is loaded,
the student presenting her report stands poised

to begin. And so she does. This day is her
second try, the first a washout due to our failed
technology. I ask, *Do you think you will earn*

another chance each time error is out of your hands?
This day, a new day, she stands confident,
prepared for questions from her peers, the one

question she's noted that I ask of them all—
What is it that this artist has allowed you
to achieve? This day, I forget the other

questions I always wait to ask. This day, they ask
no others, just stare outside at the lot
of parked cars, play with the ends of their hair.

They want to hear voices that give them reason
to listen. They want the blare of car horn,
tires screeching without a final thud. They

want a lecture, a formula that does it all,
a recitation of the method that always gets
things done. And one woman says it, that she

is sad, and all of them nod, and another says
that she is angry, too. And how could they
not indict. And why won't justice ever be

served. And why won't anyone do anything
to change the America in which we live. And
I look at my classroom—the Brown, the Black,

and the white of my room—and I ask who
it is that must make the change we need.
And they talk about the Government. They

talk about the System. They talk about our
Economics. And our Judges. And our Juries.
They. And they tell me of their lives, their fears,

their boyfriends and their fathers, our illness
and our poverty, their rights and their desires,
how none of us are ever safe. And the room

becomes their last surrender while they wait
for me to teach. I say, *This is the part where
you wait for me to synthesize your words*

then tell you what to do. And every face
grows hopeful, just as we all did the night
before, before we knew what we've always

known, that knowing the truth doesn't save
us. And I take a sip of water and tell them
every true thing that I know—that they are

the power who will save what needs saving,
then answer their next questions with more
and more questions, asking until time is up.

WE PUT SO MUCH FAITH IN THE POWER OF DOORS

Yes, we heard it would storm but we'd heard it before—
how we should buy water and board up our windows,
test out our flashlights, and stock up on gas.

What is it you need when you're fleeing your home?
When you're hungry and frantic, in need of clean
clothes? When the neighborhood's empty and they've shut

down one bridge, toll takers dismissed in the darkening
swirl? You pack up the puppies. You water
your plants. Throw clothes in a suitcase. Drive away . . .

then turn back. You think for a minute. Take your checkbook
and cash. Grab your meds and your papers. Pack
some photographs, too. Snag those cheese enchiladas, a bottle

of wine. Those student assignments you've still yet
to grade. Some textbooks. Your journals. Eyeglasses.
Your keys. And then you stand watching, just looking

around—at the TV, the sofa, the CDs—your life.
The wood floor you swept last just that afternoon.
Your backyard. Your front yard. This high tide. This sea . . .

CRUISE TO NOWHERE

Someone tell me what to pack, when we aren't going anywhere

and staying there too long. This is a journey of philosophers,

an epistemological study of where we could be and why not.

I will bring those shoes that feel as though I am bare-

foot, the sturdy bra made of delicate lace and elastic, the dress that was

a skirt that is a coat and folds up to be its own carrying case.

I will dance the last night with sea-foam legs, and eat the Astroturf.

This is my chance to not get away from it all, to be on board

but not bored, to experience the meaning of the journey,

the conceptual reality of the verb. I will sail, like a boomerang.

I will learn how it feels to be well on my way to no real destination,

to exit from the finger traps, to counter every pull. And when

we've returned, yes, I'll notice the change from the woman I once was

before I went nowhere to this very moment, and this one, and this . . .

BATHWATER

It is moving day and we are running around in concentric circles, zeroing in on our departure from this place. We've had enough of surveying the aftermath, the sand and silt of what remains when low tide returns and the ocean recedes, leaving these streets to cough and choke on wreckage. The newscasters report the medial view—the watermark lines, the overturned cars, but with no grave departure from the straight-ahead gaze.

News flash: the seagulls and pigeons are falling from the sky. Feral cats drowned, remain stiffened on the sidewalks, bloated next to clamshells. All our vision is peripheral.

Downstairs, the workers take a lunch break, remove their masks to bite their sandwiches, down long swigs of their beers, tell crude jokes to one another. They will tear down the sheetrock. Pull up the floorboards. Throw away the canned goods, everything in our garage. They will make this place better than they found it, better than it ever was. They are creating hidden alcoves to store the seasonal things. There will be a room beneath the flight of stairs for what a family chooses to keep on hand but not encounter every day.

Upstairs, the movers create a line of assembly—boxes, furniture, bed frames. Our mattresses sail down the stairs like life rafts. In one room, there are needles in a corner on the floor requiring someone's comment. One of us says something linking lazy kids with diabetes. The movers keep it fluid; they've seen it all before, honor us with silence.

This is trash. This is going. This is to be stored until we have the core strength to decide. This pile was never ours. We don't know how it got here and we don't know where it goes.

Your grandmother learns that things fall from the sky and come into your bedroom at night. This is the legacy she leaves us all: when your strength is insufficient to protect you, allow the mind to create an alternative world where you are the permanent victor. There are those who understand this logic, without question—rescued, feral animals; the core of silenced women; the children made to play alone. A world inside a world is still a world apart. What this means to your mother is that it is her job to be watchwoman, to secure the locks to all the windows and doors, be ready to traverse realities, take action at any time. Your mother uses sharp words and poisons to erode the locks on sticky doors. She stands at the thresholds and curses out enemies, walks on broken glass, points out blood puddles on the floors. Notice continuity—the outside seeping in, the changing face of bondage, the omnipresence of intrusion. This is your life we are living. Continue to pare down this cautionary tale . . . *There once was a woman who lived in a house and survived on her own. There once was a woman who lived in a house, and survived. There once was a woman who lived . . .*

ORNITHOLOGY

She could have been their mother. God, how long had it been
since they'd seen her last, left her nest for the longer flights?

They'd found another home with other wildlife, surrounded
by water and swampy lands. Angled eaves stood in for trees.

And it worked. Even more than humans, they belong where they are.
They are a natural resource. They are allowed to fly free.

They'd grown into adults, and so it all made sense, the ratio
of size and the speed with which she flew toward them.

She was and used the wind. She drew them into herself
with the fury of a mother reunited and consumed, allofeeding

all her babies, allopreening all her flock. The rock dove. The osprey.
Allogrooming all their feathers until nothing living remained.

━

Captain Sully was called a hero for saving all those souls. A miracle
that he ditched that aircraft, engine failure due to bird strike.

AFTERMATH

I see it now.

There is not enough room in the apartment to keep things that I will not use. Here, in these closets, there is no clear space for Someday, no basement or attic for Just In Case. In this new residence, everything must pull its own weight—be in working order, be a benefit to me now, and have a designated spot to call home.

I think about the notion of memorabilia all the time—tickets from movies I attended and paid for, autographed books I no longer want to read. I struggle with the thought that what I may discard will not be a part of my life anymore and wonder what will happen if I need what I no longer have.

I look around my compact Brooklyn apartment, in a neighborhood I love, and try to find a home for items with some degree of potential. An overlooked area for Maybe One Day, a hidden corner to store In the Event I Should Move Again. And it's true. I can choose to keep such things: the box for my Tiffany-like lamp shade, the Holy Bible now spotted black with mold. The choice to grip and hold on is always there, but it is a choice with consequence. It is done so with the risk of displacing the present and the future with some distorted vision of the potential of my past.

I examine all that I've salvaged from the wreckage. It is too much to take in right now. I create another stack of things to sort through when I can.

HOLDING

We come from all over and gather here,
settle into this space, so near the set
but not yet of it. There is no quiet here,
just bravado and its fatigue, excitement
and its thirsty hunger. There is always a man
that you've seen somewhere before,
somewhere you can't recall, and this
is no déjà vu . . .

        It is time to find a place
at the table. Union gets first choice,
the seats nearest whatever is deemed
to matter most—the door, the food,
the next necessary steps leading
to an easy exit when all the paperwork
is done. A faux cop saunters over—
asks if I was on that overnight shoot
last Tuesday, tells me I should save
my time, it isn't worth the hassle
for the way our kind is treated.

        Our kind—
we are a single lot in here, pulled into the mix
for the ways we add without distracting,

provide a wash of color without our edges

too defined. And this somewhere is where

the background lives—in this very gym,

this opulent ballroom, this church meeting

hall, sporting carry-on after carry-on, garment

bag after garment bag, each one of us

portraying someone who comes alive

when standing before the cameras, mouthing

conversations, most charming in a silent crowd.

BOARDING THE SIX TRAIN AT BROOKLYN BRIDGE

When we board early at the end of the line,
we have all the choices in the world—to grab
a window in the two-seater bench, to sit near
the door for a quick escape, to opt to face
backward on the forward moving train.

But some of us may choose to stand, may choose
to satisfy that crave to sway and be swayed, revel
in the herky-jerk of the drowsy conductor, lean
on the closing doors despite everything we know.

We are passengers on this local line, wedged
into seats too small for our frames, determined
to neither touch nor be touched—to maintain

our gaze without seeing, our joy without
smiling, our thoughts without speaking,

our lives without taking a breath.

NO MATTER WHAT THE INCLINE,
THE RIVER AROUND US STILL FLOWS

When we walk along a trail, we are walkers
on that trail. It sounds so simple, to be that
which we do, simply because we do it. And
if we walk alongside pilgrims, we too take
on pilgrimage, seek our own something, take

to our own path. The pilgrims say *Bonjour* to me,
and *Bonjour* I respond. They say *This part*
of the journey is steep for us, yes? and I say *Yes,*
it is. I am a pilgrim on my way to insight and isn't
that the truth? This group climbs so fast, leaves me

in the dust. When I lose sight of them, I take a new
left, meander through the village. After the potter,
at the street's end, stands the old church with all her doors
flung open. And here come those pilgrims, from the one
other way, standing in the lengthening queue, behind me.

The ways. The means. The final destination.

PRIMATE

How long after one leaves the bathroom
does one cease to be someone
who has just left the bathroom,

who has set aside the morning
spreadsheet and algorithms to take
a break from genius to genus?

The body is so insistent, in full command
of who we are and what we do, until it is not.

Several times each day, we are reminded of ourselves
and do what every other animal does, without
a need to pretend there is no need.

We drink our water. We urinate.
We eat our food. We defecate.

If someone shared the human way with us, we clean
ourselves, blot and wipe, flush, observe, adjust.

We check our closures, seams, and trails.
Our image in the glass.

We soap and rinse away our under-selves—the ones
who wail when pain commands, protect our own,
identify our alphas, let nature rule our runts.

THE DEATH AND THE DYING,
A MILLION TIMES OVER

The stories we repeat the most are the ones
that survive the years. Every year, those left
in this village enact the flood and the fleeing,
the women who were washing clothes, soon
so much of life scrubbed clean. They remember

the blessings of the priest, the fishermen's boats
in the harbor, the houses of ill repute. Every
year, they perform for themselves, for all
who will come, the tale of the potter's work,
how his children toiled late into the nights

that you and I need never eat from our tables
and drink from our own cupped hands. They
show how to make ropes to knot everything
taut, how to carve stone that will last. And,
every year, it ends with a marriage and a dance.

What he did. What she did. The forecasts of wind.

IT IS HAPPY HOUR, SOMEWHERE

I am in our bed, pregnant and bleeding through this day's dusk. The obstetrician ordered bed rest, but I am getting hungry, call out to you beyond the closed door into darkness. And everything is dark, muffled and thick, resounding with silence, and so I walk away from our bedroom to find you.

There is no other place for you to sit other than where you are, on the floor, your feet straight out before you, your back against a wall. You are rocking, front to back. You are on the telephone. You tell her that you love her. You tell her she can keep it. You tell her that she doesn't have to have an abortion if this is something that she does not want to do.

You do not see me. I focus on the many layers of vision—what the intelligent mind understands, what the open spirit knows. Every day, I wait for the miracle of recognition.

My body begins to tell a generational tale. You tell her to hold on, tell me to get back in the bed. I am pregnant and bleeding and lean against the nearest wall, walk the hallway at an impossible angle without lights or map or footnote.

I have told all the world that when life presents choices, I will choose you. You, above my five senses and truth. You, above family, friends, all others. I declared *Divorce* an expletive, to be unspoken in our home. I am pregnant and bleeding and there is no light in this bedroom—no table lamp for reading, no illumination overhead. They have been an afterthought because one of us is blind and one of us can't see.

You come sit on my edge of the bed, hold me as I wail. *Maybe you can't have a child*, you tell me. *Maybe we can just raise hers*. You rock me, front to back, until my face feels dry to your touch. You tell me that I am done crying and then ask what it is that I want to eat for dinner.

THERE ARE SOME THINGS
WE CAN'T CREATE IN LIFE

They are standing as close as they can get to the precipice.

What she wants to feel is his arm around her
Waist, pulling her back from the edge.

This is the water ballet they enact—the tension
And the release, withholding in order to forgive

And be forgiven.

There is a wedding party to their left, taking
Photographs in gown and tux, yellow slickers
Over their fanciness. He says, *Posing is such a charade.*

And she thinks how, years later, those photos
Will fade into their truth, no one recalling being
Told to turn toward the light and flash a smile

With teeth showing.

He pictures himself upstream and floating,
Where even these currents can't force him to move.

One of them is cheating on a husband.
One of them is cheating on a wife.

What it is that he wants, he never says.

THERE ARE SIXTY-FIVE STEPS
BETWEEN THERE AND HERE

And, no matter how you count it, sixty-five steps
are never that far, never that much of a stretch away
from being a manageable count, no matter the terrain,
no matter what the weather. After sixty-five steps, you
can look back, still make out your starting point, gold pin

on the map of your past. This is something you know you
can do. I've checked my pedometer, new app on my old
phone, know now for a fact—you can go around the world
ten times, not exceed this humble number. You can walk
into the ocean, cup hands around the sea. You can live

and breathe a million miles, make lefts and rights galore,
before that double-six appears, if it ever appears to us at all.
And, if our steps are numbered, may this be our cosmic pass,
our do-over free ride toward life's completion, our one good
long stint to try once again, to reset and do this thing right.

The old way. It's windstorm. The new way. It's breeze.

THE ONLY TIME WE THINK OF IT
IS WHEN IT'S NO LONGER THERE

On the blueprints, it's a patio—not a playground, not a park.
No fountains here to quench the thirst between rounds of tag
or hopscotch. When one must drink, one goes upstairs, risks
being kept inside. And so, one chooses to live parched
and does this all the summer. Our generation sucked on ice,

well, it lasted so much longer than Dixie cups of H_2O,
or washcloths dripping water. We waited for that first hot day,
those green-clad maintenance men, to crank the valves
that primed the pumps, sent water to the sprinklers. They were
our heroes, wrench in hand, these men who made the rain

so we could shriek, and mess our hair, our playclothes soaked
till see-through. But go upstairs for bathing suits? Risk angry
disapproval? Our mothers, they would look at us, see work
to do upon us. So we would stand there, tongues stuck out,
take in every drop we could. Our flip-flops fixed

to this one sweet spot, the whole wide world around us.

BAY ONE

Today it is all about mystery cocktails and G-strings,
the woman with the full bar set up across three blankets,
taking cash, cards, Venmo, and Apple Pay. Topless is a morning
option, bottomless, a late afternoon dare. Next to us, three
boys take in our sandy family time, comment on my lipstick,
the tilt of my floppy straw hat. *My mother would never*

be caught dead here and I wished their bond stronger than that,
I wished them all high tides, a breezy, saltwater freshness.
I watch my daughter and her wife walk into the water, my son
head off through the umbrellas to catch up with a maybe.
I think about my mother and our moments here at Riis, fifty-odd
years before. May there always be fried chicken, hot R & B on blast.

CURRENCY

Maybe you never awakened early enough, never arrived before the scruffy old man with the metal detector, his leathered wife lingering a few steps behind him, her sole task to sort found sea glass by color, and only then by shape. And even if you saw them working their way from bay to bay, you might still wonder what they do with the rest of their days, the value of their preoccupation with treasure. Their home is bought and paid for, a compact bungalow with sand swept daily from the corners of the porch, a feral tabby beneath the stairs, protective of her kittens. You will wonder why he brings home keys that open unknown locks. You will think you hear marimbas, a tenor sax, a harp; this is the sound that the sea glass might make if you go to their house and your visit is welcomed. There is sea glass in the rusting coffee tin, keeping watch in the salty, swirling air. There is sea glass in the pots of plants, jutting up from rich, deep soil. If you don't have sea glass in your home right now, how could you ever know the list of things you're missing in this life? Maybe you sleep, dream you are awake, and call this a good morning. Yes, you can do that now. Ring the bell. Step inside. Beyond the door is a sea-glass world of aqua blues and greens, everything translucent, smoothed edges turning clear.

WHAT TO DO WHEN EVERYTHING
GETS TOSSED FROM THE VESSEL

I never expected to love it so much—to drift
in a canoe with that paddle in my hands, life
jacket tight around my torso. I'd just learned
to swim, and here I was, in line with all
who had taken the course and passed along

with me. We were now all safety certified,
allowed to work our way down this river
without any other in tow. We could handle
the currents. We could flip ourselves over
and find our way up. We could swim back

to shore, in our minds. All of this, a theory,
what we practiced to remember. No one could
see beyond the last curve of the day—the sunset
in our eyes, the boulders just beneath the wild
surface, the rapids the only sound left to hear.

Cover your faces. Only breathe out. Dream you are floating away.

AND TOMORROW, WE LEARN TO NAME THE AIR

What does it mean to live where what sags
is salvaged before it falls, where what is old
is cherished and preserved? Every street
here boasts a history demanding to be retold,
every building worthy of its birth, of receiving

its own name. This house is *Maison V.* This one,
La Cebo. Back at home, so much goes without
saying. And I wonder how we escaped this joy,
content to allow a number and street name
to suffice, forgo this human need to define.

The doing. The being. Now, these structures,
objects in search of our reference, familiar
and indexed. I call this moment *The Pooling,*
this random thought *Redemption.* The bed
on which I enter sleep, *The Sweetest Yellow Plum.*

To name a thing. To give it life. To understand its meaning.

SKULLY

Move quickly through a dangerous course, avoiding opponents, or blasting them clear out of the game zone. Always seek the safety of home bases. Complete the basic level and get transformed into a being with the power to eliminate your competitors.

—Skully Central

I am sorry I flicked my bottle cap, edges up,

straight across your bedroom, so it would glide

far, but not scratch the floor. I didn't want to get us in

trouble, to do anything to bring our mothers

to the door of the room, not after their after-

noon of flowing six-packs, punch bowls, and fifths.

But there they were, holding our next

round of Cokes, the bottles shapely as all

the ladies in the living room, quenching

our thirst for attention by checking in on us.

My mother was in awe of you and your twin

sister—such beautiful blonde hair, wavy and thick,

such gorgeous gray-green eyes, skin the warm color

of well-polished pine, with outfits that never showed

wrinkles, anklets that never sank into the heels

of your shoes. And when she looked at me, her smile

dimmed as she said, Yes, that I was beautiful,

too. Even though my eyes were crossed. Even

though my thighs were thick. Even though

my knees held onto the dark and my hair had a wont

of its own. When I was six years old, I wanted

to mar the smooth surface. Forgive me this history,

this passing along of pain. I wanted to create scars

on your body, and tripped you to see where you'd land.

IN THE BEGINNING

And all along, we thought the beginning to be
that one word, but look—there are so many more,
the line and the stanza and the chapbook of words,
the shelves, stacks, and libraries lavished with words,
sentences dancing around independent clauses

on the coolest, star-filled nights. And all of them say, this
is the true beginning, and now this, and this, and yes,
even this, the rest of the night in the center of time,
a participle, dangling. You and I are commas, between
lakes and rivers and deep seas of words, the em dash

and the question, the ellipsis nearing dawn, pulled by
the moon's turn of phrase. The best lines in the world,
belly up on the beach, and we know them, toss them
back into the depths. Our lives are separated by a series
of breathing double colons. And now this, and this, and yes . . .

The simple past. The present perfect. The future continuous.

COMMITMENT

It was a risk—to remove our masks and stand
side by side, our shoulders touching for the ten-
second countdown before the shutter did its thing.

We did that with the backdrop of our elementary
school yard, empty except for its lonely portables,
and a rogue pair of restless boys, shooting the breeze.

Weeks later, we can laugh at our undue discomfort.
We lived to tell our punch line. Weeks later—and so
many thousands have died for a party, for walking

down a crowded aisle empty of paper towels and anti-
bacterial anything. I needed to hold the memory
of your smile next to mine. I needed the photographic

proof that we had found each other and corroborated
a questioned past, half a century unsure. Someone
once said that I would die in the pursuit of a touch.

I know now the dear cost of a slow-motion kiss, the vow
we would need to make to share a home-cooked meal,
a car ride on a freeway, our music loud and on repeat.

THAT WHICH WE REACH FOR
WHEN GIVEN THE CHOICE

Hasn't this always been the case—we would stand
on something solid that once felt like shore,
be calmed by the sound of water's movement,
whether trickle, rush, or wave? And even those
dreams, where tsunami would cover our landscapes

with oceans, where we would be one with the sea,
even then, the sound of the water content in itself
was the most calming crescendo of all. Yes, we know
what water knows—the rush of our blood, those
cushions surrounding each one of our cells, the inside

of insides of us. And yet, look at how we stand apart
from ourselves, choose everything other to drink. Tonight,
it's Bordeaux—that strong, heady red we pour into stemware,
to escort us away from our lives. Tonight, we raise glasses,
toast to our health, while it rains hard and threatens to flood.

ACKNOWLEDGMENTS

Grateful acknowledgment is made to the editors of the following publications, in which these poems appeared, or are forthcoming, sometimes in different versions:

AMP: "Cleansing My Mother's Cold Body," "The Garonne River Shifts Her Direction"

Belladonna/(Pre)Conceivable Bridges (chapbook): "And Tomorrow, We Learn to Name the Air," "Currency," "What to Do When Everything Gets Tossed from the Vessel," "With a View of the Water from Stable, Cleared Ground"

Belladonna/SHIRLEY (chapbook): "The Browning," "Cruise to Nowhere," "Holding," "Polar Vortex," "Quiet on the Set"

Breakwater Review: "The Death and the Dying, a Million Times Over," "In the Beginning," "No One Eats Icicles Anymore"

Chautauqua: "It Is Happy Hour, Somewhere," "Prodigal"

Crab Orchard Review: "Nine to the Limit"

Furious Flower: Seeding the Future of African American Poetry: "We Put So Much Faith in the Power of Doors"

Kweli Journal: "Skully"

Narrative: "The Only Time We Think of It Is When It's No Longer There"

Obsidian: "The Latitude, the Longitude, and a Third Axis Called Time" "What to Do When Everything Gets Tossed from the Vessel"

Poem-a-Day: "Six"

POETRY: "Socratic"

Prairie Schooner: "What We Wear to Meet the Water"

WomenArts Quarterly Journal: "Breaking & Entering"

I am grateful to the BAU Institute at the Camargo Foundation, the Yaddo Foundation, the Helene Johnson and the Dorothy West Foundation, the Virginia Center for the Creative Arts, Cave Canem Foundation, the Kimbilio Fiction Fellowship, and Adelphi University, for time and support.

With deep appreciation to Parneshia Jones, for relentlessly believing. Many thanks to Northwestern University Press and to Patrick Samuel in Acquisitions; freelance copy editor Mark Reschke; JD Wilson, Anne Strother, Emily Dalton, and Olivia Aguilar in Sales and Marketing; and Anne Gendler and Dino Robinson in Editorial, Design, and Production.

So much gratitude and love to my friends, colleagues, teachers, and students for being who you are and helping me. Deepest thanks to those who helped to make this collection come to fruition, each in their own way: Samuel Adoquei, Elmaz Abinader, Samuel Aymer, Danielle Barnhart, Judith Baumel, Frances and Gary Bixhorn, *Black Ivory*, Beverly Brown, Jason Robert Brown, Jericho Brown, Mahogany Brown, Sara Camilli, Martha Cooley, Desiree Cooper, Toi Derricotte, Anton Dudley, Ava DuVernay, Cornelius Eady, Giancarlo Esposito, Carlyn Ferrari, Jennifer Fleischner, Kermit Frazier, Heide Gardner, Erica Gimpel, Rachel Eliza Griffiths, H.R.H. Albert Grimaldi, Vashti Harrison, Randall Horton, Tyehimba Jess, Patricia Spears Jones, Tayari Jones, A. Van Jordan, Bettina Judd, Nzadi Keita, Stacy Leigh, Norm Lewis, Iris Mahan, Charlene Mayers, Abigail McGrath, Lynne and Leigh McQueen, Aimee Nezhukumatathil, Christine M. Riordan, Anika Noni Rose, Nicole Sealey, Carl Skinner, Patricia Smith, Tracy K. Smith, Marc Strachan, Ed Toney, Natasha Trethewey, Vincent Wang, Afaa Michael Weaver, Chotsani Williams West, Christian Dante White, L. Lamar Wilson, Jacqueline Woodson, Kevin Young, and Estefania Zea.

Eric Jerome Dickey, thank you for twenty-some odd years of constant encouragement, mentoring, and laughs. Rest well, dear friend. I took notes.

Thank you to my core—Dana, Winter, Anton, Linnea, and Mariel—*forever and always*.